Cats

Jill Hughes

**Illustrated by
John Francis**

NUTMEG PRESS

Designed and directed by the Archon Press Limited
70 Old Compton Street, London W1V 5PA

©The Archon Press Ltd. 1978/©This edition Shelley Graphics Ltd. 1981
Published by Nutmeg Press (A Division of Shelley Graphics Ltd.)
Printed in the United States   ISBN 0-89943-108-9

Fully-grown wild cats range in size from the tiny Rusty-spotted cat (right) which weighs less than five pounds (2 kg) to 595-pound (270 kg) Bengal Tigers (below).

2

The Cat Family

The family of cats includes animals that live in the wild as well as household pets. Pet cats—the kind you see in the streets and in people's homes—come in many colors. They can have long hair or short hair. Some have tails like thin whips. Others have thick, bushy ones. One kind of cat, the Manx, has no tail at all!

Wild cats come in many different sizes. The smallest are the flat-headed kinds that look very much like household cats. The largest are the tigers.

Cats are meat-eaters, or *carnivores*. They have strong muscular bodies, sharp senses, and dagger-like canine teeth for seizing their prey.

Of all cats, only lions live in family groups. The rest, like the cat in *The Jungle Book*, like to "walk by themselves."

The Cheetah is one of the fastest animals on Earth. It can reach speeds of 60 miles (95 kilometers) an hour. Unlike other cats, the Cheetah cannot draw in its claws. These claws act as spikes and help it to grip the ground as it runs.

3

Birth of a Kitten

Like most wild animals, household cats like a hiding place in which to have their kittens. They can usually take care of themselves very well.

The average mother cat is ready to have her kittens in about 60 to 70 days. A day or two before she has her kittens, she makes a nest for herself. She looks for a quiet, dark place, such as a closet. It is a good idea to give her a box lined with newspaper in a protected corner. She should get used to the box before the kittens are born.

At birth, the helpless kittens are licked clean by their mother. They are no more than four inches long and are completely blind at first. Their eyes begin to open after about nine days. Kittens are born with a furry coat.

A three-week old kitten standing for the first time (left).

5

Just like human young, kittens learn to care for themselves by copying their mother. One of the first habits they pick up is to lick and wash themselves.

Mother Care

The mother's care is very important in the first few weeks of kittens' lives. Her milk gives them all they need to grow strong and healthy. Until they learn to look after themselves, she regularly grooms them with her tongue.

The new mother cat must have a good diet. She needs to keep healthy to help her kittens grow. The kittens will gain weight steadily given enough good food. After about a month or so, you can introduce them to food other than milk. Give them dried milk made double strength at first. Then over the next few weeks, get them used to about four small solid meals a day.

Mother cats are very protective of their young. They will carry them away from danger by the scruff of the neck. The kittens curl into a ball when held this way. They make no attempt to struggle.

When kittens are born, the mother feeds them milk. For the first three or four weeks or so of their lives, she supplies all the food her kittens need. Her milk helps the kittens stay healthy.

6

First Steps

After nine days the kittens' eyes will open. They begin to explore their nest. At about 21 days old, kittens start taking their first wobbly steps into the world outside. Unexpected noises and movements frighten them and send them scurrying back to mother for safety.

Young kittens are such fun to play with that it is easy to think of them as toys. But they are still babies who tire easily. So don't go on playing with them if they want to curl up and sleep.

The best age to buy a kitten is after seven or eight weeks. By then it will be able to live away from its mother. But it still needs to be "mothered" by its owner. It must have a warm, clean home, regular food, and plenty of love. Your pet will learn how to use a litter box quickly if you show it how to scratch the litter with its paw.

Kittens are fascinated by the world around them. They love to play. Like wild miniature hunters, they will pounce at anything that catches their interest. Much of their time is spent stalking and wrestling each other. They are practicing the skills they will need as adult hunters.

The Great Outdoors

By the time they are five weeks old, kittens will be strong enough to follow their mother outdoors. At first they stay close to her and imitate whatever she does. But as they grow stronger, they become more independent. Soon they begin to wander.

Cats love to roam. They love to prowl all over the neighborhood. One way of teaching them to stay near home is to keep them indoors for regular periods while they are still young.

Kittens are protected against illness by their mother's milk. But they lose this protection in time. When they go outside and meet other cats, they run the risk of catching diseases. For this reason, they should be taken to the vet for shots. This should be done after they are about two and a half months old.

Outside, your kitten faces many dangers. If it gets caught in a tree or on a roof, try tempting it down with strong-smelling fish. Cats have no sense of traffic, so keep them away from busy roads. They also don't have nine lives—that's just a folk tale!

When buying kittens, make sure they have healthy bodies, firm limbs, and thick, shiny coats. Check that their eyes are clear and healthy-looking, too.

12

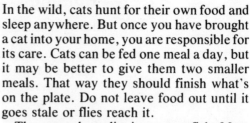

Bed and Board

In the wild, cats hunt for their own food and sleep anywhere. But once you have brought a cat into your home, you are responsible for its care. Cats can be fed one meal a day, but it may be better to give them two smaller meals. That way they should finish what's on the plate. Do not leave food out until it goes stale or flies reach it.

The general cat diet is meat or fish. Most modern brands of cat food (canned, dry, or moist) will give your cat all the vitamins and minerals it needs. Follow the feeding instructions on the labels.

Cats should have plenty of fresh water. This is very important if your cat eats a lot of dry food. Sardines and liver are rich in vitamins. They are a good addition to a healthy diet, but only every so often.

Cats like to be fed on a regular basis. Young kittens should be fed baby cereals twice a day. They also need one or two other meals of meat or fish.

Your cat will need to have its own bed or basket. A cardboard box lined with newspaper is good. Keep this box out of drafts and in a cozy corner. The kitten will sleep there at night. But by day, it will find a warm, sunny spot to stretch out in.

13

Hunting

Kittens, just like lion and tiger cubs, learn to hunt by watching and imitating their mothers. In fact, much of their play is a kind of pretend-hunting.

Pet cats stalk their prey just like their cousins in the wild. They use bushes or tall grass as a cover until they are near enough to pounce. They crouch low with their tails swishing from side to side in excitement, waiting for the right moment. With a sudden rush, they spring onto their victim, biting the back of its neck to kill it.

A domestic cat that returns to the wild will mostly hunt small animals such as mice and birds. But it might also go for fish, frogs, and even spiders and insects. Sometimes cats will even chew grass. This helps their digestion.

Cats seem to enjoy hunting. Even well-fed cats will hunt from time to time. But unlike wild cats, they like to play with their catch. They trap it and let it go over and over again, rather than eat it right away.

Pet cats often give their uneaten prey to their owners, as gifts. The owners are usually far from happy!

The cat skeleton

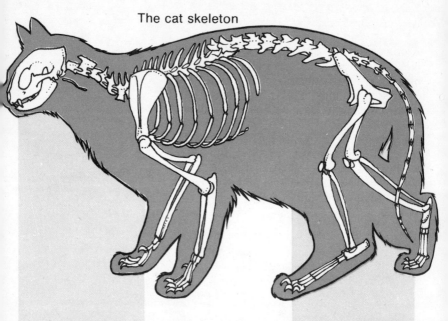

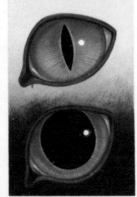

In bright light, the pupils of a cat's eyes narrow to a thin slit. When the light is dim, they widen to let in as much light as possible.
A cat's eyes have a sheet of reflecting tissue behind them. At night, when light falls on them, the eyes can be seen to shine.

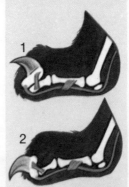

1

2

The Cat Machine

The cat's skeleton is amazingly flexible. Its 230 or so bones are held together by more than 500 muscles. Some of the most powerful lie around the neck and shoulders. These are used to strike and kill. Others at the lower back and hind legs are powerful also. These are used for jumping. As the cat leaps, its hind legs uncoil like a spring. The body seems to stretch to almost twice its original length.

A cat does not walk with its feet flat on the ground. It walks on "tiptoe." Only the small rough pads of skin on the bottom of its feet touch the ground.

At the end of each toe is a claw that is attached to tendons in the leg. When the tendons are relaxed, the claws stay almost hidden (1) in side a protective sheath, making it easier for the cat to walk. When a cat tenses its tendons (2), the claws are extended. Claws are used for climbing, scratching, and catching prey.

2

Cat Feats

Cats are great athletes. There are many stories about their amazing feats, but some are hard to prove. Folk tales about a cat's nine lives give a good idea about their uncommon ability to survive.

Domestic cats can manage a good burst of speed, at least for short distances. From a crouch, most can easily jump 10 feet (3 meters) high. They can also leap distances many times their own length.

The Van cats of Turkey are famous for their love of water. Yet most cats can swim if they have to. During World War II, a ship's cat survived an attack. It was fished up from the Irish Sea. The cat had been swimming for a long time. Cats also have a good sense of direction. They have been known to travel many miles to return to their old homes.

Cats are very limber. Watch how a cat washes itself. Then try turning your head around far enough to lick your back!

Dropped upside down, a cat first turns its front legs 180 degrees (left), then its hind legs to land with all four feet on the ground.

Cats are good jumpers (right). Their hind legs are longer than their front ones. They are powerful enough to send a cat upward to many times its own height.

19

Mongrel and Pedigree Cats

A cat is a pedigree animal only if it has five generations of purebred ancestors. Very few of the pets you see are pedigrees. About 13 million cats are born in the U. S. each year. Of these, no more than half a million are pedigree cats. The rest, like the handsome black and white cat (left), are mongrels, or mixed.

Domestic cats are grouped according to the length and color of their coats. Mongrels, or mixed breeds, can have kittens of many different colors with many different markings. Pedigree cats will have kittens that look very much like themselves.

Pedigree cats, like this Cream Burmese (right), have been specially bred for their shiny coat colors and their good looks.

The Brown Tabby is
one of the most
popular of pets. Its
rich brown coat has
black markings.

The Tabby

All the cats on the next pages are pedigree animals. They have been specially bred to get exact colors and markings.

The Tabby in the picture belongs to a group with thick bodies and rounded heads known as British Shorthairs. The Tabby's fur has markings that form a striped or blotched pattern. These are either black or a darker shade of the color of the coat. The name Tabby comes from a kind of silk with similar markings made in Iraq.

Some people think that all domestic cats have tabby-like ancestors. Many modern cats surely do show the ring-tailed markings of Tabbies.

Tabbies can be long-haired or short-haired. Their coats range from silver to brown and red. Many have a dark "M-shaped" mark on their foreheads.

Wild cats in Europe have tabby-like markings. A cat like this may have been the wild ancestor of modern Tabbies.

23

The Abyssinian

The Abyssinian cat of today looks very much like the cats in ancient artwork from Egypt. Some people think that it may come from them. This cat has a short, light brown coat. The ends of its fur are shaded with dark brown or black bands called "ticking." The Abyssinian is a Foreign Shorthair cat. It has a head shaped like a wedge, slanted eyes, and a slim body.

Cats have always been special to people. They were often thought to have special powers. In ancient Egypt, cats were worshipped as gods. In life, they were treated very well. After death, they were often prepared as mummies. Sometimes they were given bowls of milk for their trip into the world of the dead.

The Abyssinian is the
oldest known
purebred cat of all. It
first became popular
in the 1880's.

25

The Siamese

Chocolate-point

Lilac-point

Siamese cats are probably the most famous of the Foreign Shorthairs. Their strange good looks and great intelligence have made them a favorite subject for stories and movies.

Siamese cats have slim, muscular bodies, delicate wedge-shaped heads, and deep blue slanting eyes. Their feet, legs, and tails have dark markings known as points. So do their faces and ears. Different kinds of Siamese are named after the color of these points. The most common is the Seal-point. It has a creamy coat and points of dark seal brown. There are also Chocolate-point, Blue-point, and Lilac-point. More rare breeds are the Tabby and Tortoiseshell-point Siamese.

According to legend, they were the palace cats of the court of Siam for at least 400 years before they became known in the rest of the world.

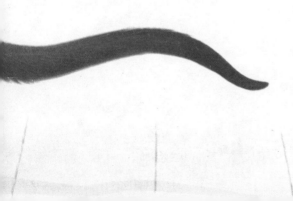

Siamese, like the Seal-point at left, are very active and friendly animals. Unlike other cats, they easily take to walking on a leash. Siamese are also very noisy. Owners can often overhear them talking to themselves and to the world in general!

27

Long-haired Cats

Long-haired pedigree cats have round, wide heads, flat faces, and full cheeks. Their bodies are stocky and their legs are short. They come in almost every color. The thick, silky fur of these cats is their most attractive feature. People sometimes call them Persians. Yet all officially known long-haired cats have actually come from the Angora cat of Turkey.

The coats of long-haired cats need a lot of care. They should be brushed or combed daily to get rid of tangles and loose hairs. Otherwise, the cats will swallow some when they wash themselves. This may lead to balls of hair forming in their stomachs. A vet's care might then be needed.

The green eyes and rich, silvery coats of Chinchillas make this breed one of the most beautiful in the world. They are rare and very hard to breed.

Russian Blue

Tortoiseshell

Coats of Many Colors

Nearly all cats are covered with a rich layer of fur. But the coats of domestic cats no longer look like those of their wild cousins. Years of breeding have brought about a wide range of different colors and markings.

The graceful Russian Blue, once called the Archangel cat, has a glossy blue coat like a seal's. In pedigree cats, the entire coat has one color, and it has no other markings. The eyes are bright green.

In contrast, the coat of the Tortoiseshell cat is very colorful. It is covered from head to tail in bright patches of black, light red, and dark red. It often has tabby markings, too. Pedigree Tortoiseshells are very rare and hard to breed. Almost all are females. This is one of the strange outcomes of breeding animals to get special features.

The Manx cat (right) is an unusual breed that has no tail at all. It is said that the Manx was late for the Ark and Noah accidentally slammed its tail in the door. Having no tail does not stop the Manx from running and jumping as well as any other cat.

Can You Speak Cat?

Cats can be noisy creatures. They purr, growl, meow, hiss, and make all sorts of other sounds. These noises are kind of a language. They have a meaning for other cats. They are also used to talk to other animals, and to people, too.

Most cat owners soon learn to understand what their pet is saying when it meows loudly near the food dish. In time, other sounds also take on meaning, too.

Cats also "talk" with their bodies. The looks on their faces, the angle of their tails, and the way they hold themselves all tell something. They tell if cats are relaxed and happy, a little annoyed, or angry, and ready to lash out with their claws.

Understanding your cat takes patience. But it is well worth the effort. As you and your cat become used to each other, a bond of friendship will grow between you.

Cats make loving house pets. But, no matter how house-trained, cats never really lose their urge to go prowling about on their own.

32